Tools

Search

Notes

Discuss

MyReportLinks.com Books

Go!

ENDANGERED AND THREATENED ANIMALS

THE BLUE WHALE

A MyReportLinks.com Book

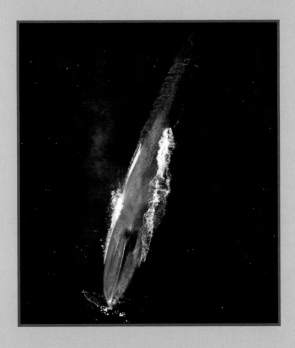

Chris Reiter

MyReportLinks.com Books

an imprint of

 Enslow Publishers, Inc.

Box 398, 40 Industrial Road
Berkeley Heights, NJ 07922
USA

MyReportLinks.com Books, an imprint of Enslow Publishers, Inc. MyReportLinks is
a trademark of Enslow Publishers, Inc.

Library of Congress Cataloging-in-Publication Data

Reiter, Chris.
  The blue whale / Chris Reiter.
     p. cm. — (Endangered and threatened animals)
  Summary: Discusses what blue whales are, why they are endangered, what
  their current status is, and what is being done to help them. Includes
  Internet links to Web sites related to blue whales.
  Includes bibliographical references and index.
  ISBN 0-7660-5055-6
  1. Blue whale—Juvenile literature. 2. Endangered species—Juvenile
literature. [1. Blue whale. 2. Whales. 3. Endangered species.] I.
Title. II. Series.
  QL737.C424 R45 2002
  599.5'248—dc21
                            2002003747

Printed in the United States of America

10 9 8 7 6 5 4 3 2 1

To Our Readers:
Through the purchase of this book, you and your library gain access to the Report Links that specifically back
up this book.
The Publisher will provide access to the Report Links that back up this book and will keep these Report Links
up to date on **www.myreportlinks.com** for three years from the book's first publication date.
We have done our best to make sure all Internet addresses in this book were active and appropriate when we
went to press. However, the author and the Publisher have no control over, and assume no liability for, the
material available on those Internet sites or on other Web sites they may link to.
The usage of the MyReportLinks.com Books Web site is subject to the terms and conditions stated on the
Usage Policy Statement on **www.myreportlinks.com**.
In the future, a password may be required to access the Report Links that back up this book. The password
is found on the bottom of page 4 of this book.
Any comments or suggestions can be sent by e-mail to comments@myreportlinks.com or to the address on
the back cover.

Photo Credits: BBC News, p. 23; © Corel Corporation, pp. 3, 10; Dan Shapiro, National Oceanic
and Atmospheric Administration/Department of Commerce, Sanctuary Collection, p. 24;
DiscoverySchool.com, p. 16; John Bavaro, p. 21; Mike Johnson/earthwindow.com, p. 1;
MyReportLinks.com Books, p. 4; National Oceanic and Atmospheric Administration/Department of
Commerce, NOAA's Ark Collection, p. 42; NOAA, National Marine Mammal Laboratory, p. 20;
NOAA, Pacific Marine Environmental Laboratory, p. 31; PBS, *Nature*, pp. 18, 40; PBS, *Secrets of the
Ocean Realm*, p. 27; The Endangered Species Coalition, p. 34; The Marine Mammal Center, p. 12;
The Monterey Bay Aquarium, p. 15; The National Aquarium in Baltimore, p. 38; The National Parks
Conservation Association, p. 29; The United States Fish and Wildlife Service, p. 43.

Cover Photo: Mike Johnson/earthwindow.com

Contents

MyReportLinks.com Books
Great Books, Great Links, Great for Research!

MyReportLinks.com Books present the information you need to learn about your report subject. In addition, they show you where to go on the Internet for more information. The pre-evaluated Report Links that back up this book are kept up to date on **www.myreportlinks.com**. With the purchase of a MyReportLinks.com Books title, you and your library gain access to the Report Links that specifically back up that book. The Report Links save hours of research time and link to dozens—even hundreds—of Web sites, source documents, and photos related to your report topic.

Please see "To Our Readers" on the Copyright page for important information about this book, the MyReportLinks.com Books Web site, and the Report Links that back up this book.

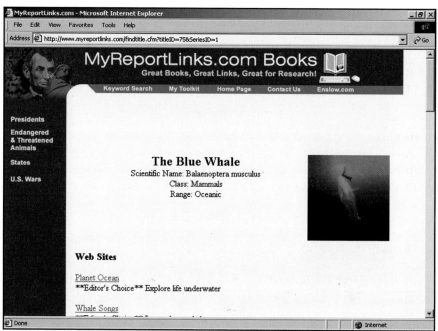

Access:

The Publisher will provide access to the Report Links that back up this book and will try to keep these Report Links up to date on our Web site for three years from the book's first publication date. Please enter **EBW1825** if asked for a password.

Report Links

The Internet sites described below can be accessed at
http://www.myreportlinks.com

*EDITOR'S CHOICE

▶ **Planet Ocean**

"Planet Ocean" offers an exploration of underwater life. Here you will
learn about some of the ocean's creatures, including the blue whale, the
barracuda, and other interesting marine life.

Link to this Internet site from http://www.myreportlinks.com

*EDITOR'S CHOICE

▶ **Whale Songs**

The Whale Song Web site provides information about cetaceans,
including the blue whale, the humpback whale, the sei whale, and
other whales. You will also find a trivia section where you can test
your knowledge about cetaceans.

Link to this Internet site from http://www.myreportlinks.com

*EDITOR'S CHOICE

▶ **Endangered Species**

The Endangered Species Web site provides information about
endangered species all over the world. Here you will find the endangered
species list, a list of conservation organizations, facts about species, the
texts of laws and policies, and much more.

Link to this Internet site from http://www.myreportlinks.com

*EDITOR'S CHOICE

▶ **American Cetacean Society Fact Sheet**

At the American Cetacean Society Web site you will find fact sheets
on the blue whale and other whale species. Each fact sheet provides an
in-depth physical description and information about each species.

Link to this Internet site from http://www.myreportlinks.com

*EDITOR'S CHOICE

▶ **Marine Mammal Center: Blue Whale**

At the Marine Mammal Center you will find a brief description of the
blue whale and information about its habitat, behavior, mating and
breeding habits, and endangered status. You will also find links to
information about other marine mammals.

Link to this Internet site from http://www.myreportlinks.com

*EDITOR'S CHOICE

▶ **Species Information**

At the U.S. Fish and Wildlife Service Web site you will find links to the
Endangered Species Act, the Federal list of endangered and threatened
wildlife and plants, and other resources on endangered species.

Link to this Internet site from http://www.myreportlinks.com

  The Internet sites described below can be accessed at
http://www.myreportlinks.com

▶ **Acoustic Monitoring**
At this Web site you will learn about a study being done to monitor marine
animals through acoustics. By navigating through the site, you can listen
to whale vocalizations and learn about the biology of the blue whale and
other whales.

Link to this Internet site from http://www.myreportlinks.com

▶ **Amazing Animals: Blue Whales**
This Web site features a brief discussion about the blue whale, including
"amazing facts" about its size, habitat, and diet.

Link to this Internet site from http://www.myreportlinks.com

▶ *Balaenoptera musculus:* **Blue Whale**
At this Web site you will find information about the blue whale's habitat, diet,
and physical characteristics. Included are images of the blue whale.

Link to this Internet site from http://www.myreportlinks.com

▶ **Baleen Whales**
Commonly asked questions about baleen whales and the answers are a feature
of this site. Find out, among other things, why baleen whales were hunted for
so many years.

Link to this Internet site from http://www.myreportlinks.com

▶ **Blue Whale**
This Web site offers some of the reasons the blue whale population has
declined and includes research and recovery plans for the world's largest
living mammal.

Link to this Internet site from http://www.myreportlinks.com

▶ **Blue Whale**
At the National Aquarium in Baltimore, you will find information about
some well-known species including the blue whale and the humpback whale.

Link to this Internet site from http://www.myreportlinks.com

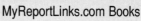
Report Links

 The Internet sites described below can be accessed at
http://www.myreportlinks.com

▶**Blue Whale**
The National Parks Conservation Association Web site has brief
profiles of endangered and threatened species, including the blue
whale. It also lists national parks where blue whales can be found.

Link to this Internet site from http://www.myreportlinks.com

▶**Blue Whale: *Balaenoptera musculus***
At this Web site you will find a fact sheet on the blue whale that
includes information about its life span, range, and other assorted facts.

Link to this Internet site from http://www.myreportlinks.com

▶**Blue Whale: *Balaenoptera musculus***
This Web site provides an overview of the blue whale, including a
physical description, its endangered status, range, habitat, and other
interesting facts.

Link to this Internet site from http://www.myreportlinks.com

▶**Cetacea**
This Web site provides information about whales, dolphins, and
porpoises, all members of the same order of marine mammals. In
particular, you will find out about the effects humans have had on
these species.

Link to this Internet site from http://www.myreportlinks.com

▶**Climate Row Touches Blue Whales**
This article from the BBC examines the effects of global warming on
the decrease in krill, the blue whale's main source of food, and the
possible effects on the arctic blue whale population.

Link to this Internet site from http://www.myreportlinks.com

▶**Endangered Species Act**
This Web site describes how the Endangered Species Act works. You can
learn here how a species gets listed and what a "candidate species" is.

Link to this Internet site from http://www.myreportlinks.com

Report Links

The Internet sites described below can be accessed at
http://www.myreportlinks.com

▶**Endangered Species Act of 1973**
The United States House of Representatives Committee on Resources Web
site contains the complete text of the Endangered Species Act of 1973.

Link to this Internet site from http://www.myreportlinks.com

▶**Marine Mammals**
The Monterey Bay Aquarium provides profiles on several marine mammals
including the blue whale, the gray whale, the humpback whale, the sperm
whale, and others.

Link to this Internet site from http://www.myreportlinks.com

▶**Marine Mammal Protection Act (MMPA) of 1972**
At the Office of Protected Resources Web site, you will find the text of the
Marine Mammal Protection Act of 1972 and an overview of the act's features.

Link to this Internet site from http://www.myreportlinks.com

▶***Nature:* Humpback Whales**
PBS's *Nature* series explores the humpback whale. Here you will learn about
the habits of humpbacks, the songs they sing, and facts about whales in
general. You will also find additional online resources about whales.

Link to this Internet site from http://www.myreportlinks.com

▶***Nature:* Monsters or Mermaids?**
At this PBS Web site you will find a brief article about manatees, the marine
mammals that gave rise to the legend of the mermaid.

Link to this Internet site from http://www.myreportlinks.com

▶**Office of Protective Resources**
At the Office of Protective Resources Web site, you will find the texts of the
Endangered Species Act, the Marine Mammal Protection Act, and other
documents and speeches. You will also learn about recent efforts to protect
endangered species.

Link to this Internet site from http://www.myreportlinks.com

Report Links

▶ The Internet sites described below can be accessed at
http://www.myreportlinks.com

▶ Phillip Colla Photography
By navigating through this Web site you will find an assortment of
beautiful underwater photographs of whales, dolphins, seals, sea lions,
manatees, sharks, rays, fishes, and other marine life.

Link to this Internet site from http://www.myreportlinks.com

▶ Sea Dwellers
This PBS Web site, *Secrets of the Ocean Realm*, provides information
about the blue whale, the gray whale, southern right whale, the
humpback whale, and the sperm whale. You will also find information
about other animals that live in the sea.

Link to this Internet site from http://www.myreportlinks.com

▶ Species at Risk: Blue Whale
This site provides an overview of the blue whale and offers details
about the threats facing these creatures. It also describes Canada's
attempts to protect the blue whale.

Link to this Internet site from http://www.myreportlinks.com

▶ Whales
At the Defenders of Wildlife Web site you will find several articles
about whales, including one about Japan and whaling and an
article about the effects of climate change on whales.

Link to this Internet site from http://www.myreportlinks.com

▶ Whale Net
Whale Net provides extensive information for students, teachers, and
the public about whales. Here you will find satellite tagging data,
Internet resources on whales, and an e-mail section that lets you send
questions about whales to a scientist.

Link to this Internet site from http://www.myreportlinks.com

▶ World Wildlife Fund: Endangered Species—Blue Whales
The World Wildlife Fund Web site provides a brief overview of the blue
whale. It also lists some of the factors that have contributed to the
decline in the blue whale population as well as those that may have
helped in its recent recovery.

Link to this Internet site from http://www.myreportlinks.com

Blue Whale Facts

Class
Mammalia

Family
Balaenopteridae

Genus
Balaenoptera

Species
musculus

Average Length
70 to 100 feet (21 to 30 meters); females about 5 percent longer than males

Average Weight
100 to 120 tons
(91 to 109 metric tons)

Life Span
Over 80 years

Status
Listed by the United States Fish and Wildlife Service (USFWS) as endangered on June 2, 1970.

Skin Color
Bluish-gray and mottled with gray and white; underside yellowish or whitish

Teeth
Baleen (whalebone) strips extending from 270 to 395 plates in the jaw

Breeding Season
Midwinter months

Gestation Period
11 to 12 months

Offspring
One every 2 to 3 years

Range
Worldwide; separate northern and southern stocks

Maximum Speed
Over 19 mph (30 kph)

Threats to Survival
Hunting by humans, habitat loss, pollution, competition with humans for food

Voice
Low, rumbling, often arranged in patterns

Spout
Up to 30 feet (9 meters) high

The World's Largest Animal

Imagine the largest animal ever to have lived on earth. Imagine a creature so big it weighs more than ten full-grown elephants. Imagine a heart the size of a compact car and a gargantuan mouth that devours the equivalent of about 32,000 quarter-pound hamburgers in a single day.[1] Now that's an appetite!

A creature so big, with an appetite so enormous, surely has to be the hulking, meat-eating *Tyrannosaurus rex* or the towering *Apatosaurus*. But in fact, the world's largest animal ever is not an extinct dinosaur. It is alive today, swimming in all the world's oceans. It is the giant of the sea, the blue whale.

Just how big is the blue whale? Let's go back to that heart. It's as large as a small car because it must move blood the entire length of the whale's long, streamlined body, an astonishing 100 feet (30 meters). It would take twenty schoolchildren lying end to end in a straight line to equal the length of the blue whale. An average first-grader could actually crawl through the whale's aorta, the large artery that carries blood from the whale's heart to the rest of its body. Each beat of the blue whale's heart pumps 60 gallons (227 liters) of blood into the aorta![2]

▶ A Limited Diet

Such a huge animal needs a lot of food to keep it going. One might think that a blue whale would eat a few big fish every day to satisfy its hunger. But the whale's diet is made up almost entirely of a tiny, shrimplike creature called krill.

Trying to get full on krill is like trying to make three square meals out of a swarm of gnats—one would need to eat a lot of them. That's just what the blue whale does. During its six-month feeding season in the cold polar seas, it devours 40 million krill every day—an amazing 8,000 pounds (3,629 kilograms) of krill![3] This is a very, very big animal.

The blue whale's size gives it many advantages. Large animals stay warm more easily than small ones and tend to expend less energy feeding. Blue whales also have few predators. Killer whales, also known as orcas, sometimes attack young blue whale calves, but mature blue whales are

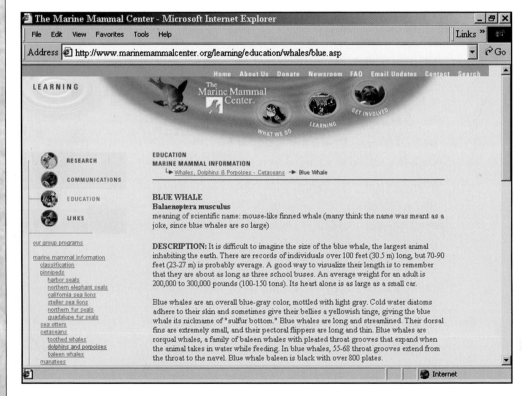

The blue whale, the largest animal on earth, is an endangered species despite its size—and because of it: One blue whale provides much more blubber, whalebone, and oil than several smaller whales.

rarely threatened. Even fierce sharks stay away from the mighty blue whale.

Their great size also gives blue whales a powerful voice. They make deep, rumbling sounds that travel for hundreds of miles across the ocean. The sound is something like that of a foghorn or a tuba played underwater. Scientists believe that the blue whale's calls are a way of communicating with other whales. As blue whales search for krill, for instance, a resounding bellow may tell other whales where to find a good meal.

An Easily Spotted Prey

Unfortunately, great size has its disadvantages, too. For centuries, ocean hunters coveted the blue whale. When they spotted a big blue whale swimming the open seas, they saw an unmatched source of meat, oil, and whalebone. Before electricity, whale oil was burned in lanterns to provide light. Whale meat was an important part of the diet of many people. Whalebone was used in corsets and umbrellas. Whalers could make a profit from selling those products. But the early whalers were no match for the powerful, swift-swimming blue whale. Their open rowboats were too slow, and their hand-held harpoons too weak. Late in the nineteenth century, however, whalers began to use fast, steam-powered boats, harpoon cannons, and exploding harpoons. By 1900, whalers were killing thousands of blue whales each year. In 1931, more than 29,000 blue whales were killed in a single season.[4]

The Effects of Whaling

Modern commercial whaling nearly wiped out the world's population of blue whales. Scientists estimate that a population of 250,000 that lived before whaling began was

reduced to less than 10,000.[5] Some believe the numbers dropped as low as 2,000.

Ten thousand whales might sound like a lot. But whalers killed almost three times that number in a single season. That is why blue whales are an endangered species—a species that is in danger of becoming extinct.

▶ The International Whaling Commission

Blue whales have been considered an endangered species since 1966. They had become so scarce by then that the International Whaling Commission (IWC) declared an end to the hunting of the great whale. The IWC is the agency responsible for the regulation of the whaling industry and the conservation of whales.

The United States is a member nation of the IWC. In addition to following the IWC ban, the United States has passed laws that protect whales and other species at risk.

In 1972, Congress passed the Marine Mammal Protection Act, which banned fishing for all whales, dolphins, and porpoises in U.S. waters. And in 1973, Congress passed the Endangered Species Act, which combined and strengthened the provisions of earlier endangered species acts. It provides for the conservation of all domestic and foreign animal and plant species that are endangered. Once a species is listed under the act as endangered or threatened, that species receives protection under the law. Along with listing the blue whale, the act listed seven other species of whales that had been hunted to near extinction: the gray whale, bowhead whale, fin or finback whale, humpback whale, northern right whale, sei whale, and sperm whale.

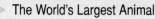

Tools   Search   Notes   Discuss   Go!

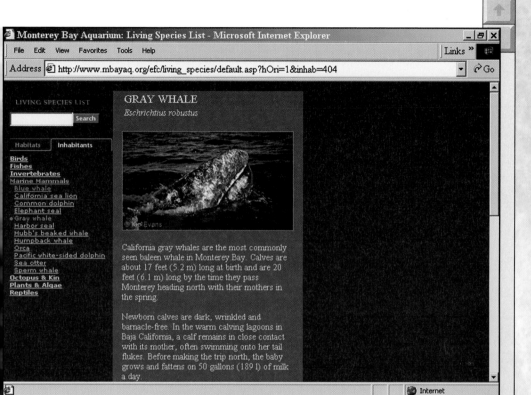

Monterey Bay Aquarium: Living Species List - Microsoft Internet Explorer

File   Edit   View   Favorites   Tools   Help   Links »

Address http://www.mbayaq.org/efc/living_species/default.asp?hOri=1&inhab=404   Go

LIVING SPECIES LIST

Search

Habitats | **Inhabitants**

Birds
Fishes
Invertebrates
Marine Mammals
  Blue whale
  California sea lion
  Common dolphin
  Elephant seal
● Gray whale
  Harbor seal
  Hubb's beaked whale
  Humpback whale
  Orca
  Pacific white-sided dolphin
  Sea otter
  Sperm whale
Octopus & Kin
Plants & Algae
Reptiles

GRAY WHALE
Eschrichtius robustus

© Kip Evans

California gray whales are the most commonly seen baleen whale in Monterey Bay. Calves are about 17 feet (5.2 m) long at birth and are 20 feet (6.1 m) long by the time they pass Monterey heading north with their mothers in the spring.

Newborn calves are dark, wrinkled and barnacle-free. In the warm calving lagoons in Baja California, a calf remains in close contact with its mother, often swimming onto her tail flukes. Before making the trip north, the baby grows and fattens on 50 gallons (189 l) of milk a day.

Internet

△ *Once listed as an endangered species, the gray whale has recovered in recent years and is no longer considered endangered.*

▷ **Hopes for Recovery**

Today, whales are enjoying a modest recovery. The population of gray whales has recovered so well that they are no longer considered endangered. You can even watch gray whales migrate off the west coast of North America. They swim from the shores of the Baja California peninsula in Mexico all the way north to Alaska. Many blue whales follow a similar route. They can be seen during the summer and autumn in the waters off the central California coast. Scientists have counted up to 2,000 blue whales there. It is the largest concentration of blue whales in the world.[6]

Chapter 2

What Makes a Whale a Whale?

Given their enormous size, it is hard to imagine that whales are closely related to humans. But both whales and humans are mammals, animals that breathe air and have well-developed brains and warm blood. Female mammals produce milk to nourish their young. A mammal has two

Blue Whale - Planet Ocean - DiscoverySchool.com - Microsoft Internet Explorer

File   Edit   View   Favorites   Tools   Help   Links »

Address http://school.discovery.com/schooladventures/planetocean/bluewhale.html   Go

For Students
For Teachers
For Parents
Favorites
Brain Boosters
Clip Art Gallery
Puzzlemaker
Science Fair Central

Planet OCEAN • The Ocean • Blue Whale • Tubeworm • Barracuda • Marine Megastars

BLUE WHALE

Everything about the blue whale is enormous. It is the largest animal on earth, ever. A big blue whale can be 100 feet long and weigh up to 150 tons. That's as large as a Boeing jet. Its heart is as large as a small car. Fifty people could stand on its tongue. Its spout shoots up at least 30 feet when it surfaces for air.

CLICK FOR AMAZING FACTS!

How do whales breathe?

A whale's "nostrils" are called blowholes and are on the top of its head. Some whales have one blowhole and others, like this blue whale, have two. Unlike humans, whales breathe voluntarily. That means they choose when to take a breath. This is important because whales can't breathe underwater. They surface every few minutes to blow out a mixture of water and air and take in a breath of fresh air.

Done   Internet

▲ Both blue whales and humans are mammals. But unlike humans, who breathe involuntarily, blue whales "choose" when to breathe. A blue whale must surface from the ocean every couple of minutes to expel water and take in fresh air through the two blowholes on top of its head.

layers of skin: the top layer, or dermis, and the bottom layer, or epidermis. The sense of touch exists over a mammal's entire body, and most of a mammal's other sense organs are located in its head. There are about five thousand different species, or individual types, of mammals.

▶ Mammals of the Sea

Most mammals have a coat of hair all over their bodies. But some mammals, those that live at least some of the time in the water, do not have much hair at all. These are the marine mammals.

There are three main groups of marine mammals: pinnipeds, sirenians, and cetaceans. Seals, sea lions, fur seals, and walruses are all pinnipeds. Of the three groups, pinnipeds have the most hair because they spend a lot of time on land as well as in the water, usually in colder temperatures, and they need hair for warmth as well as for protection from being cut by rocks.

The sirenians, or sea cows, make up the second group of marine mammals. These peaceful animals spend almost all of their lives in shallow coastal waters or rivers. Sirenians eat underwater plants and grow to be quite large. The largest sirenian, the Steller's sea cow, was known to grow up to almost 25 feet (8 meters) in length, but it is now extinct. The other sea cows, the manatee and the dugong, are also increasingly rare.[1] The manatee, which can grow up to 13 feet (4 meters) long and weigh up to 1,300 pounds (590 kilograms), lives along the southeastern coast of the United States as well as in coastal waters off Central America, the West Indies, northern South America, and western Africa. Dugongs are found in the tropical and subtropical waters of the Indian and Pacific Oceans, but most are found in the waters off Australia.

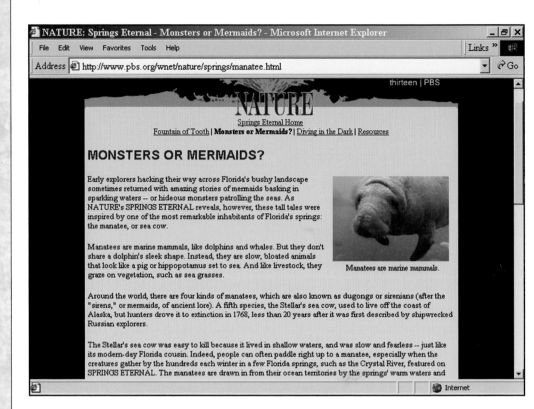

NATURE: Springs Eternal - Monsters or Mermaids? - Microsoft Internet Explorer

File   Edit   View   Favorites   Tools   Help   Links »

Address: http://www.pbs.org/wnet/nature/springs/manatee.html   Go

thirteen | PBS

NATURE

Springs Eternal Home

Fountain of Tooth | **Monsters or Mermaids?** | Diving in the Dark | Resources

MONSTERS OR MERMAIDS?

Early explorers hacking their way across Florida's bushy landscape sometimes returned with amazing stories of mermaids basking in sparkling waters -- or hideous monsters patrolling the seas. As NATURE's SPRINGS ETERNAL reveals, however, these tall tales were inspired by one of the most remarkable inhabitants of Florida's springs: the manatee, or sea cow.

Manatees are marine mammals, like dolphins and whales. But they don't share a dolphin's sleek shape. Instead, they are slow, bloated animals that look like a pig or hippopotamus set to sea. And like livestock, they graze on vegetation, such as sea grasses.

Manatees are marine mammals.

Around the world, there are four kinds of manatees, which are also known as dugongs or sirenians (after the "sirens," or mermaids, of ancient lore). A fifth species, the Stellar's sea cow, used to live off the coast of Alaska, but hunters drove it to extinction in 1768, less than 20 years after it was first described by shipwrecked Russian explorers.

The Stellar's sea cow was easy to kill because it lived in shallow waters, and was slow and fearless -- just like its modern-day Florida cousin. Indeed, people can often paddle right up to a manatee, especially when the creatures gather by the hundreds each winter in a few Florida springs, such as the Crystal River, featured on SPRINGS ETERNAL. The manatees are drawn in from their ocean territories by the springs' warm waters and

Internet

▲ Manatees, who live in shallow coastal waters and rivers, belong to the group of marine mammals known as sea cows. Of the three species of manatees alive today, two are endangered and one is threatened.

The sea cows, despite their size, are so graceful that many believe the legend of the mermaid is based on them.[2]

Whales, dolphins, and porpoises belong to the third group of marine mammals, the cetaceans. There are seventy-eight known species of cetaceans, and probably more that we do not know about.[3] Though the characteristics of cetaceans vary greatly, they all have the same general body shape, which is basically rounded and larger at the front than at the back. They also all have nostrils on the tops of their heads, no hind limbs, and a flat horizontal blade at the end of their tails, making them nimble swimmers.

Marine biologists who have touched cetaceans say their skin is usually very smooth.[4]

▶ Toothed Whales

Less pleasing to touch is the equipment in a cetacean's mouth. Sixty-seven species of cetaceans have teeth and are therefore called "toothed whales." All dolphins and porpoises are in this group, as are several types of whales.[5] These animals survive in the water by hunting fish and squid that are much smaller—usually between a hundred and a thousand times smaller—than they are.[6]

▶ The Blue Whale and Other Baleen Whales

The remaining eleven whale species make up a class all their own. They are called baleen whales, and they do not have teeth. Instead, they have long strips of bone, called baleen, along the insides of their mouths. Baleen is made of keratin, which is a substance like that of human fingernails.[7] The baleen changes in size from the back to the front of the jaw, with the outermost strips being fine and flexible, like the bristles of a broom or brush. In fact, when whales were commonly hunted, their baleen was used to make just these things.[8]

Baleen whales are filter feeders. When they are feeding, they swim through shoals, or large groups, of prey. They take in enormous gulps of water, which they then expel through their baleen, capturing thousands of krill, the small, shrimplike creatures that form most of their diet.[9]

Krill occur in "astonishing abundance" in the cold Southern Ocean (an ocean formed by the southern portions of the Atlantic, Pacific, and Indian Oceans), where they are also eaten by certain seals, penguins, squid, and fish.[10] They can grow to be two-and-a-half inches

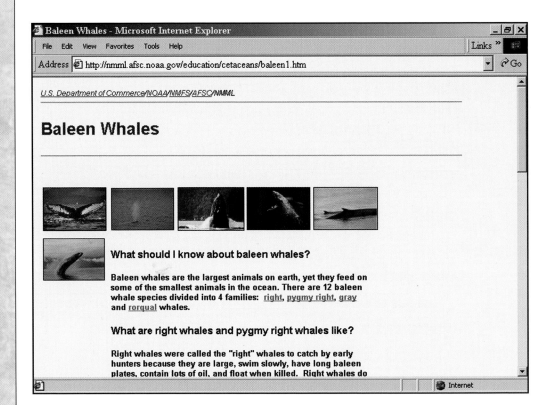

Baleen Whales - Microsoft Internet Explorer

File   Edit   View   Favorites   Tools   Help   Links »

Address   http://nmml.afsc.noaa.gov/education/cetaceans/baleen1.htm   Go

U.S. Department of Commerce/NOAA/NMFS/AFSC/NMML

Baleen Whales

What should I know about baleen whales?

Baleen whales are the largest animals on earth, yet they feed on some of the smallest animals in the ocean. There are 12 baleen whale species divided into 4 families: <u>right</u>, <u>pygmy right</u>, <u>gray</u> and <u>rorqual</u> whales.

What are right whales and pygmy right whales like?

Right whales were called the "right" whales to catch by early hunters because they are large, swim slowly, have long baleen plates, contain lots of oil, and float when killed. Right whales do

Internet

▲ *Blue whales are baleen whales—instead of teeth, they have long strips of bone in their mouths called baleen that filter water and strain food.*

(six-and-a-third centimeters) in length, which is between a million and a hundred million times smaller than the whales that eat them.[11]

▶ The Rorquals

Seven types of baleen whales are referred to as the rorquals. These whales have a series of pleats, or grooves, running along their throats and bellies. The name "rorqual" is from the Old Norse *rorhval*, meaning "grooved whales."[12] The individual species of rorqual whales are the humpback, fin, sei, Bryde's, minke, pygmy blue, and blue whales.

The blue whale, *Balaenoptera musculus,* is the largest of the rorquals. Females are generally larger than males of the same age, and the largest known blue whale was a female killed in the late 1920s near the South Shetland Islands, off the tip of the Antarctic Peninsula. She was an astonishing 109 feet 4 inches (33 meters 10 centimeters) long. The largest male came from the same waters at around the same time. He was 107 feet 1 inch (32 meters 3 inches) long.[13] Even the largest dinosaurs would have looked small standing next to those creatures.

Blue whales are named for their color. The tops of their heads, backs, and tails are blue to bluish-gray, sometimes with gray patches. Their bellies are lighter, usually yellow-ish or whitish, and the undersides of their bellies are white. Blue whales are sometimes called "sulfur-bottoms" because a small film of algae that grows on their undersides reflects bright yellow.[14] Their baleen, which grows from almost 400 plates on each side of the upper jaw, is black. The

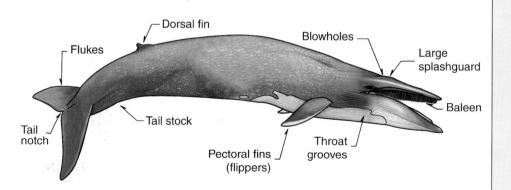

▲ The blue whale features grooves along its throat and belly, paired blowholes, a pointed snout, a small dorsal fin, and black baleen plates. It is so named for its color, which is light bluish-gray above, mottled with gray or white, and a sometimes yellow belly, caused by a film of algae.

longest known fibers of baleen have measured almost 4 feet (1 meter) long.[15]

In the water, a blue whale is usually easy to tell from other whales. Besides its color, its size gives it away. You can be pretty sure you are looking at a blue whale if the animal is longer than 75 feet (23 meters)—a good deal longer than an average school bus. Blue whales can weigh up to an immense 150 tons (136 metric tons).[16]

The pygmy blue whale, a variant of the blue whale, was first written about in 1961. It is most commonly seen in the Southern Ocean, especially in the Indian Ocean near the Kerguelen Islands. Even though "pygmy" implies a small size, female pygmy blue whales can reach a length of almost 80 feet (24 meters), and males about 70 feet (21 meters).[17]

▶ Krill and the Blue Whale Migration

Wherever there are oceans, there are whales. Blue whales are found worldwide in two separate groups that do not interbreed. One group lives in the northern seas, and the other group lives in the southern seas. Although some whales stay in the same general area for their entire lives, blue whales migrate, traveling long distances between feeding and wintering waters.

Blue whales spend the summer months of each year in frigid polar seas. The northern stocks migrate to the Arctic region, and the southern stocks swim to the Antarctic. This movement is tied to the polar food bloom, when krill are plentiful and multiplying.[18] Blue whales feed intensively during these months, gorging on krill and putting on lots of weight. As much as one ton of food has been found in a blue whale's stomach during the peak of the feeding season.

Krill are the tiny shrimplike creatures that serve as the main food source for the enormous blue whale. Conservationists are now concerned that global warming is causing ice melts in the seas where krill live and blue whales feed, further endangering the species.

Krill do not reproduce in the exact same spot every year, but blue whales seem to be able to use their powerful voices to let one another know where to feed. Once they find a shoal of krill, blue whales have several ways of making the krill swim closer together so they can swallow more krill in each mouthful. Blue whales sometimes dive beneath the shoals and swim in circles, releasing bubbles as they go. As the bubbles float upward, they confuse the krill, who react by swimming closer together for protection. Then the whales swim through the center of the group and eat many, many krill.[19]

Scientists are not sure why the krill just do not swim through the bubbles, but the whales' feeding style is so effective that it is called "bubble netting." Scientists have observed teams of whales working together to form very large bubble nets. When whales work together like this, it is widely believed that they coordinate their actions with special sounds.[20]

Krill usually have little luck trying to swim away from whales, though, because whales are fast swimmers. While feeding, whales swim from 1 to 4 mph (2 to 6.5 kph) and their normal cruising speed while migrating through the open ocean is between 3 and 8 mph (5 and 14 kph). When pursued or wounded, whales have been known to swim up to 20 mph (30 kph)![21] After taking a deep breath on the

▲ These blue whales are seen surfacing in the waters of the Gulf of the Farallones National Marine Sanctuary, just north of San Francisco, California.

surface, a whale can dive into the ocean and stay beneath the surface for twenty minutes or more.[22]

▶ Breeding Grounds

As winter comes and the polar food bloom ends, blue whales migrate thousands of miles to their breeding grounds, where whales couple and mate. Even the whales that are too young or too old to breed make the annual migration.

Once fertilized, a female blue whale carries her young for ten to eleven months. She seeks out calmer, warmer waters to give birth, and does so in midwinter.[23] A fertile female blue whale usually gives birth to one infant, called a calf, every two to three years.

Like all mammals, blue whale calves nurse on their mother's milk. For the first few weeks of their lives, they can gain up to 250 pounds (113 kilograms) daily, just from drinking milk! Because a lot of milk is lost into the water during the process of nursing, female whales sometimes produce up to 750 pounds (340 kilograms) of milk each day.[24]

Away from the polar waters, blue whales do not eat that much. Even their biggest gulps of food amount to no more than a tiny snack when compared to the huge mouthfuls of krill they swallow while in the icy polar waters. Because they store so much energy, blue whales and other baleen whales can fast, or go without eating, longer than most any other animal.[25] Then as spring approaches, they are ready to head north again, continuing the migratory rounds they have made for thousands of years.

Chapter 3 ▶

Whaling and Other Threats

Humans have hunted whales for their meat and oil since before written history. The Alaska Native people, among other native people living in Arctic lands who traditionally hunt whales, have done so for three to four thousand years. They still use boats called *umiaks* made of sealskin stretched on a wooden frame.

In the past, once the whale was pulled ashore, the Alaska Natives would gather for many hours to pray and thank the whale for giving its life. It was then butchered, and the blubber, meat, and bones were all used—no parts of the whale were wasted. Only a few whales were killed each year, and the overall population of whales remained healthy.[1]

▶ Whalers of the Past

The Norwegians have also eaten whale meat for thousands of years, although it is not known whether they originally hunted or scavenged for whales. The Japanese, too, have a long history of whaling, with written records of whale hunts dating back to 1606. The first European whalers were the Basques (people from the western Pyrenees Mountains, along the border of France and Spain), who were known to hunt whales in the Bay of Biscay as far back as the tenth century. These early hunters used small, simple boats to track and chase whales. They would thrust a harpoon into a whale's back, and the whale would exhaust itself dragging the hunters' boat. The whalers would eventually pull alongside the tired whale and stab it with a long metal lance, hoping to puncture its heart or lungs.[2]

▶ Modern Whaling

During the second half of the nineteenth century, the methods and instruments used to hunt whales changed dramatically. In about 1864 a Norwegian named Svend Foyn invented a cannon that could be fixed onto the bow, or front, of a ship.[3] The cannon fired harpoons farther and faster than they could be fired by hand.

Right whales got their name from whalers because they were considered the "right" whales to hunt—they were plentiful, easily caught, and did not sink. Southern right whales are more abundant than northern right whales, which are the most endangered whale species, with fewer than 1,000 remaining.

The cannons were mounted on steam-powered ships, allowing whalers to reach the polar seas where whales congregate to feed each year. Whalers also learned that a whale could be pumped full of air to keep it from sinking. Before that discovery, whalers could only hunt whales that floated. But now whalers could hunt most any whale and easily transport it back to port for processing.

Over the years, whalers established processing sites closer and closer to whale stocks. They also built factory ships on which they butchered, processed, and froze whales while still at sea. The factory ships would anchor near large icebergs, which blocked the fierce weather, while small boats called catchers did the actual hunting. When a catcher boat killed a whale, it towed it to the factory ship for processing. Technology was transforming traditional whaling into a fast-growing industry.

With advanced technology, whaling became even easier. Whalers began to use helicopters and other aircraft to spot whales from above. They also tracked whale movements with sonar, a device that uses the echoes of underwater sound waves to locate objects. When whalers discovered that a certain frequency of sonar caused whales to panic and surface, many ships began using that frequency.

Other modern whaling methods included the use of exploding harpoons, from which pieces of metal were blasted throughout a whale's body by an explosive charge in the harpoon's tip. When people became concerned that these explosions were wasting too much meat, whalers began to use cold harpoons. These were blunt metal tubes that could knock a whale unconscious, or possibly kill it, if they were fired into exactly the right spot. Whales were usually struck by several cold harpoons before they died.[4]

Polluted Seas

But whalers were not the only threats to whales. Many chemical products made by humans have been found to be extremely harmful to marine life, and they are still finding their way into ocean waters. Some of the most harmful chemicals are compounds known as organohalogens, which are commonly found in pesticides, insecticides, herbicides, and fungicides. While many organohalogens are no longer produced, they are still being released into the environment when disposed of improperly.

One type of organohalogen, polychlorinated biphenyl (PCB), is a fairly common pollutant. When whales feed

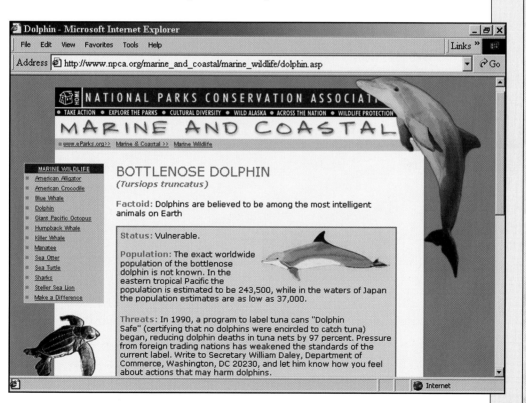

▲ Other cetaceans are accidentally killed when they are caught in fishing nets. Dolphins are sometimes caught in nets intended to catch tuna.

29

on small animals with PCBs in their tissues, the chemical accumulates in the whales' flesh in very high levels. That accumulation can lead to serious health problems for whales, affecting their ability to have offspring and weakening their immune systems. Even though PCBs are no longer produced, many nations still use existing supplies.

▶ Commercial Fishing

Many cetaceans also lose their lives each year in "accidental killings" when they get caught in fishing nets. Dolphins, for example, get caught in nets intended to catch tuna because tuna often swim beneath dolphins, following them to sources of food.

Even greater numbers of cetaceans are believed to have drowned in drift nets, which are now banned worldwide by a United Nations declaration.[5] Drift nets are nearly invisible and highly flexible nets that trap any marine animal larger than the holes in the nets' mesh. Before being banned, drift nets were being used to catch more fish than any other method of fishing. These nets were secured on either end by floats and sometimes extended up to 60 miles (96 kilometers). They were cast out at night, when the fish could not see them, and collected the following morning. In addition to catching nontarget fish, which were simply thrown away, drift nets accidentally killed hundreds of thousands of marine mammals each year as well as large numbers of seabirds and sea turtles.[6] Unfortunately, despite the ban, illegal fleets still use drift nets on the high seas.

▶ Other Threats to Whales

Whales face many other threats. They often die from collisions with seagoing vessels. Both large ships and small fishing boats can do serious harm to whales.[7] Of course, the reverse is also true—whales have been known to do serious damage to ships, even sinking some of them.

Coastal development can also affect the lives of whales. Building that goes on in coastal areas causes small particles of sand and dirt, or sediment, to run off into the ocean. Sedimentation clouds the water, cutting off sunlight and changing the flow of nutrients in the sea. Sometimes it changes the marine environment so much that coastal waters can't support many forms of aquatic life. Whales may depend on these life-forms. And when development

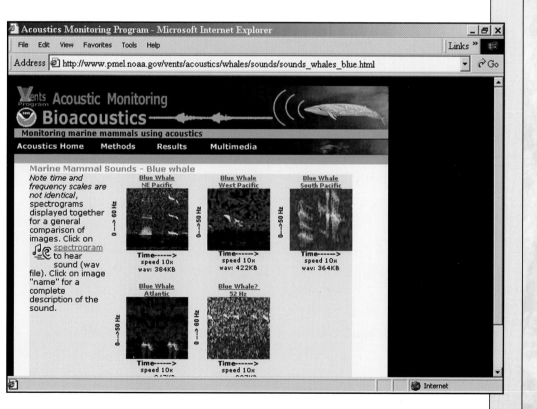

When artificial sounds are added to the seas, researchers believe whales, who use sound to navigate, are further threatened.

along the coast brings too many people to whale breeding grounds, whales have been known to avoid those areas.

Underwater noise is another cause for concern. Researchers believe whales use sound to navigate. When sonar, underwater explosions from military testing, and the drone of underwater oil wells add strange new sounds to the sea, whales can become confused. Some scientists suspect that whales beach themselves on shorelines when underwater noise interferes with their navigation.

▶ Whales in the Web of Life

Every creature in the ocean has a purpose, even if we do not yet understand it, and all marine life is somehow interconnected. Some scientists have compared this relationship to the parts of a spider's web, with each species being a strand of the web. When one strand is damaged, the strands that are connected are also harmed. If too many strands are frayed, the whole web may fall apart.

When we take too many creatures from our oceans, we run the risk of damaging the web of life. Many people realized this as they saw whales hunted to near extinction. They decided to do something about it.

Chapter 4 ▶

The Growing Concern for Whales' Welfare

Whales began to receive legal protection in 1931, when the League of Nations, an international assembly, passed the Convention for the Regulation of Whaling. This protected some whale stocks, giving special consideration to those whales most endangered at the time—the gray, bowhead, and right whales. Not all countries adhered to the restrictions on hunting those whales, but most countries began to honor the hunting ban in 1937, when the convention was made law. Some hunting of gray and bowhead whales by aboriginal peoples—the original inhabitants of an area—was still permitted.

The outbreak of World War II gave whales a bit of rest, because whaling in many areas ceased altogether. Many whaling vessels were torpedoed as countries fought over territory in the seas. In 1946, after the war, when whalers returned to the seas, the International Convention for the Regulation of Whaling was ratified in Washington, D.C. That same year, the International Whaling Commission (IWC) met for the first time.

▶ An End to Blue Whale Hunting

The IWC began to monitor and regulate whaling worldwide, but in its early years, the organization acted more to develop the whaling industry than to protect whales. By 1964, the total population of blue whales hovered under two thousand, and many people feared that the species would soon disappear from the earth.

In 1966 the IWC finally called for the end of blue whale hunting. Certain whaling countries, however, did not enter into the agreement. Peru and Chile, for example, continued hunting blue whales.

During the 1970s the IWC began to more actively protect whales.[1] At the same time, the United States passed two laws that increased protections for all cetaceans. The first law was the 1972 Marine Mammal Protection Act, which banned fishing for whales, dolphins, and porpoises in U.S. waters and made it illegal to import whale products into the United States. This feature of the act was

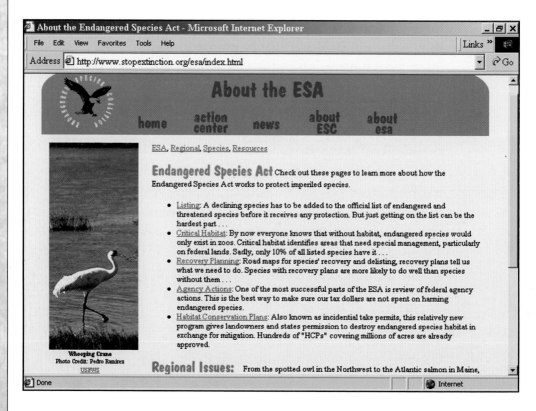

The Endangered Species Act of 1973 established protections for animal and plant species considered endangered or threatened. Blue whales are among six whale species whose status is currently endangered.

important because whale oil was still being used to manufacture machine oil and cosmetics.[2]

The second was the Endangered Species Act, passed by Congress in 1973, which established special protections for animals and plants in danger of disappearing from the earth. The act also protects "threatened species," those species considered likely to be in danger of extinction if they are not protected. Blue whales and seven other whale species were listed by the act as endangered.

▶ Commercial Whaling Moratorium

In 1982 the IWC passed its boldest whale conservation action ever. It proclaimed a moratorium, or temporary halt, on all commercial whaling, beginning in 1985. During the moratorium, which continues today, the IWC has been reviewing its management policies to decide whether some whaling can be conducted at levels that will not devastate the future of the species.[3]

The IWC has no direct power to force nations to follow its rules. But many member nations have threatened economic sanctions against those countries that continue to hunt whales. Sanctions are measures that block trade with a country, which can affect its economic well-being. The United States has repeatedly threatened sanctions against nations that break IWC rules, but has rarely imposed sanctions over whaling concerns.[4]

The IWC rules allow nations to issue themselves permits to kill whales for scientific research. Japan, Iceland, and Norway have issued themselves such permits, and continue to be criticized by the international community for doing so. Many conservationists see the permits as a way to get around the whaling moratorium, because many of the research programs in those countries have not

fully met IWC standards. There are also other effective methods of research that do not involve killing whales.

▶ The Argument for Conservation

Conservationists believe that whaling must be stopped in order to prevent whales from becoming extinct. And when a species becomes extinct, all other species in an ecosystem are affected. Conservationists also argue that killing whales is unnecessary because there is no longer any need for products made from whales. There are good substitutes for whale oil, whalebone, and whale meat. Moreover, they say, killing whales is inhumane—it causes great pain to a magnificent creature for no reason.[5]

There are also people against whaling who believe it is good business to promote healthy whale stocks. The total amount of money spent by people who travel out onto the oceans hoping to see whales has far surpassed the total money spent on whale products. One researcher found that in 1992, almost 3.5 million Americans and nearly 5 million people worldwide went on whale-watching expeditions.[6] But even the best intentions can have negative effects. The popularity of whale-watching expeditions has led to some collisions between boats and whales, and the increased traffic on the seas has harmed whales and other marine life in other ways. The United States National Ocean Sanctuary Program has issued strict guidelines designed to protect whales and other marine creatures from overzealous sightseers.

Chapter 5 ▶ Current Status of Worldwide Whale Populations

There are fewer than 10,000 blue whales in the oceans today, far fewer than swam the seas before modern whaling began. The gray whale population is small, too. Gray whales have vanished from the Atlantic Ocean, and though they have recovered enough worldwide to be removed from the endangered species list, gray whales are now found only in the Pacific Ocean. There, they number only about 20,000.[1] Without strong conservation measures, both blue whales and gray whales may not survive long into the future.

Of the other whales, the northern right whale is the most endangered. There are fewer than 1,000 of these whales swimming in our oceans. Despite being protected, they are showing few signs of recovery and are very rare in the eastern North Atlantic and North Pacific Oceans. The southern right whale, though not as endangered, has still greatly decreased in number. There are about 7,000 southern right whales today. There were between 60,000 and 100,000 before the species was hunted.[2]

There are only about 8,500 bowhead whales, but that species is showing signs of recovery.[3] At the time of the commercial whaling moratorium in 1986, the number of bowhead whales had dropped to about 7,000, just over half of their population before they were widely hunted.[4] Some subsistence hunting of the bowhead is allowed, but the number of whales killed each year is low, and recovery has not been affected. (Subsistence hunting of a species is

▲ Scientists believe there are fewer than 10,000 blue whales swimming in the world's oceans today.

hunting done by people not for sport or for profit but because they depend on that species for their survival.)

The humpback whales, which are known for their elaborate songs, number around 20,000. There were originally 150,000 of these whales. While they are showing some positive signs of recovery, the humpbacks are still very vulnerable.[5]

There are currently around 65,000 sei whales and somewhere between 50,000 and 100,000 fin whales. These numbers are also well below historical levels. Neither of these endangered whale species is showing signs of recovery, but there is hope that both species will come back if measures to protect them are closely followed.[6]

Killer whales are currently in serious decline along the northwestern coast of the United States. Their numbers have dropped 20 percent in the last six years, mostly because there are few chinook salmon, their favorite prey. Killer whales, like other whales, have also suffered from contamination by PCBs. The many whale-watching boats coming into their breeding grounds may also be interrupting their reproductive processes. Conservationists are now calling on the government to protect killer whales under the Endangered Species Act.[7]

▶ Setbacks to Whale Conservation

The recovery of many whale species has been slowed by nations that continue to hunt whales despite having signed nonhunting agreements. Perhaps the worst case of this was brought to public attention after the breakup of the Soviet Union. Several former Soviet government officials admitted in the 1990s that Soviet whaling vessels had been violating the moratorium on whaling for decades and had killed thousands of whales.[8]

While Soviet ships practiced whaling in secret, a few nations have resumed whaling openly. Japan is the most prominent nation to have started whaling again. Whale meat is considered a delicacy in Japan, and scrimshaw, a type of carving done on whalebone, has long been a part of Japanese culture.

Japan defends its hunting of whales as scientific research, saying it needs to know whether whale populations are depleting the country's fish stocks. Critics say the Japanese are hunting whales because people are willing to pay high prices for whale meat. Whatever the reason,

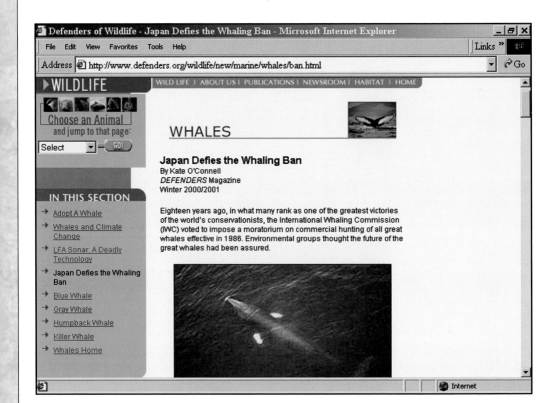

Back　Forward　Stop　Review　Home　Explore　Favorites　History

▲ Although many nations have agreed to a worldwide moratorium on commercial whaling, Japan continues to hunt and kill whales, defending its action as "scientific research."

Japanese whalers now take up to almost five hundred minke whales, forty to fifty Bryde's whales, and five to ten sperm whales each year.

Norway has killed several hundred minke whales since 1992 and still exports whale parts to Japan. This trade continues today even though it is prohibited by the international agreements Norway has signed.

At recent meetings of the IWC, there have been fierce disagreements between nonwhaling nations and those nations that want to continue hunting whales. The United States has threatened economic sanctions against both

Japan and Norway to stop their whale hunts but has not taken any action so far. In the mid-1980s, an international boycott of Iceland's fish forced that country to stop whaling, but there are signs that Iceland would like to begin whaling again.[9]

These countries are killing large whales that are protected by international agreements. But many small whales, including dolphins and porpoises, are still hunted in large numbers because they are unprotected.

Subsistence Whaling

Under IWC rules, subsistence whaling is permitted in Denmark, Greenland, the Russian Federation, St. Vincent and the Grenadine Islands, and the United States. One American Indian group, the Makah tribe of Washington State, even has a treaty with the United States government that allows the Makah to take whales. For many years, the Makah hunted gray whales, but their hunts were stopped while gray whales were an endangered species. Now that gray whales are no longer listed as endangered, the Makah hunt is again allowed. The tribe may currently take up to five whales per year.[10]

A Future for Whales

Whale sanctuaries—areas where all hunting of whales is forbidden—may be the best hope for whale recovery. The International Whaling Commission has created sanctuaries in the Indian Ocean and the Southern Ocean surrounding Antarctica. Several countries, including the United States, Australia, New Zealand, Tonga, Brazil, and the Cook Islands, have also established sanctuaries in their own waters.[11]

▲ *A big blue swims in the tropical waters of the eastern Pacific.*

There are many ways that people can help to protect whales. They can write to their government representatives and tell them that more needs to be done to protect whales. They can make changes in their everyday lives that will protect whales as well, including recycling more and throwing away less garbage so that trash will not someday end up in the oceans. They can also avoid dumping oil or other chemicals into the ground or down drains so that those products do not end up in local waterways.

Because humans are the biggest threat to whales' survival, we have in our hands the power to ensure that whales will flourish in the future. If we honor these magnificent creatures with our respect and care, they may well recover and swim the seas in great numbers as they did just two centuries ago. How wonderful it would be to look forward to seeing them for generations to come!

This series is based on the Endangered and Threatened Wildlife list compiled by the U.S. Fish and Wildlife Service (USFWS). Each book explores an endangered or threatened animal, tells why it has become endangered or threatened, and explains the efforts being made to restore the species' population.

The United States Fish and Wildlife Service, in the Department of the Interior, and the National Marine Fisheries Service, in the Department of Commerce, share responsibility for administration of the Endangered Species Act.

In 1973, Congress took the farsighted step of creating the Endangered Species Act, widely regarded as the world's strongest and most effective wildlife conservation law. It set an ambitious goal: to reverse the alarming trend of human-caused extinction that threatened the ecosystems we all share.

The complete list of Endangered and Threatened Wildlife and Plants can be found at
http://endangered.fws.gov/wildlife.html#Species

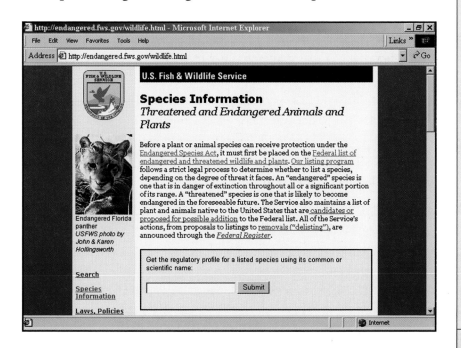

Chapter 1. The World's Largest Animal

1. Nigel Bonner, *Whales of the World* (London: Blandford Press, 1998), p. 46.

2. Roger Payne, *Among Whales* (New York: Charles Scribner's Sons, 1995), pp. 24–25.

3. "Blue Whales," *National Aquarium in Baltimore,* n.d., <http://www.aqua.org/cgi-bin/aqua/picker.pl> (3/01/02).

4. "Blue Whale," *American Cetacean Society Fact Sheet,* n.d., <http://www.acsonline.org/factpack/bluewhl.htm> (2/28/01).

5. Payne, p. 269.

6. "Blue Whales," *The Marine Mammal Center*, n.d., <http://www.marinemammalcenter.org/learning/education/whales/blue.asp> (2/28/01).

Chapter 2. What Makes a Whale a Whale?

1. Dr. Anthony R. Martin, *The Illustrated Encyclopedia of Whales and Dolphins* (London: Salamander Books, 1990), p. 10.

2. Ibid.

3. Ibid.

4. Ibid., p. 11.

5. Ibid., p. 10.

6. Nigel Bonner, *Whales of the World* (London: Blandford Press, 1998), p. 32.

7. Ibid., p. 27.

8. Ibid., pp. 37–38.

9. Martin, p. 12.

10. Bonner, p. 43.

11. Ibid., p. 32.

12. Ibid.

13. Ibid., p. 29.

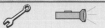
14. Ibid., p. 32.

15. Martin, p. 68.

16. Ibid.

17. Bonner, p. 32.

18. Martin, p. 68.

19. Roger Payne, *Among Whales* (New York: Charles Scribner's Sons, 1995), p. 49.

20. Martin, p. 68.

21. Ibid., p. 70.

22. Payne, p. 24.

23. Ibid., pp. 34–35.

24. Ibid., pp. 49–50.

25. Ibid., p. 51.

Chapter 3. Whaling and Other Threats

1. Nigel Bonner, *Whales of the World* (London: Blandford Press,1998), pp. 61–62.

2. Roger Payne, *Among Whales* (New York: Charles Scribner's Sons, 1995), p. 253.

3. Ibid., p. 255.

4. Ibid., pp. 254–258.

5. Ibid., pp. 303–304.

6. Ibid., pp. 304–305.

7. Ibid., pp. 173–174.

Chapter 4. The Growing Concern for Whales' Welfare

1. Roger Payne, *Among Whales* (New York: Charles Scribner's Sons, 1995), pp. 274–276.

2. Office of Protected Resources, "Cetaceans: Whales, Dolphins, and Porpoises," *National Oceanic and Atmospheric Administration,* n.d., <http://www.nmfs.noaa.gov/prot_res/species/Cetaceans/cetaceans.html> (2/10/01).

3. *Congressional Research Service Report 97–558*, n.d., <http://www.cnie.org/nle/mar-20/c.ntmh> (10/31/01).

4. Ibid.

5. Ibid.

6. Payne, pp. 222–223.

Chapter 5. Current Status of Worldwide
               Whale Populations

1. "Great Whales in the Wild," *World Wildlife Fund,* n.d., <http://www.wwf.org> (10/20/01).

2. Ibid.

3. Ibid.

4. Roger Payne, *Among Whales* (New York: Charles Scribner's Sons, 1995), p. 269.

5. Ibid.

6. "Great Whales in the Wild," *World Wildlife Fund.*

7. Energy & Environment Publishing, LLC, Natural Resources, "Northwest Orca Population in Decline," *Greenwire* (10/17/01).

8. Payne, p. 299.

9. Energy & Environment Publishing, LLC, International, "IWC Anti-whaling Stance May Soften in Future," *Greenwire* (7/27/01).

10. *U.S. Department of Commerce News*, "Fisheries Service Issues Draft Environmental Assessment on Makah Gray Whale Hunt, Sets Public Hearing," press release NOAA 01-R101 (1/12/01).

11. *CNN.com*, "Brazil approves first whales sanctuary," n.d., <http://www.cnn.com/2000/NATURE/09/20brazil.whales.enn/> (9/20/00).

Further Reading

Carwardine, Mark. *Whales, Porpoises, and Dolphins.* New York: Dorling Kindersley, 1995.

Clapham, Phil. *Whales of the World.* Stillwater, Minn.: Voyageur Press, 2001.

Cohat, Yves, and Anne Collet. *Whales: Giants of the Seas and Oceans.* New York: Harry N. Abrams, 2001.

Collard, Sneed B. *A Whale Biologist at Work.* Danbury, Conn.: Franklin Watts, 2000.

Dedina, Serge. *Saving the Gray Whale: People, Politics, and Conservation in Baja, California.* Tucson: University of Arizona Press, 2000.

Hoelzel, A. Rus, and S. Jonathan Stern. *Minke Whales.* Stillwater, Minn.: Voyageur Press, 2000.

Katona, Steven K., Valerie Rough, and David T. Richardson. *A Field Guide to Whales, Porpoises and Seals from Cape Cod to Newfoundland.* Washington, D.C.: Smithsonian Institution Press, 1993.

Miller-Schroeder, Patricia. *Blue Whales.* Orlando, Fla.: Raintree Steck-Vaughn, 1998.

Morton, Alexandra. *In the Company of Whales: From the Diary of a Whalewatcher.* Custer, Wash.: Orca Book Publishers, 1999.